THE REBELLION BEGINS

THE REBELLION BEGINS

WESTBOROUGH AND THE START OF THE AMERICAN REVOLUTION

By Anthony Vaver

PICKPOCKET
PUBLISHING
Westborough, MA
www.PickpocketPublishing.com

ISBN: 978-0-9836744-4-3

Library of Congress Control Number: 2017954624

Pickpocket Publishing

41 Piccadilly Way, Suite 202

Westborough, MA 01581

http://www.PickpocketPublishing.com

Although the author and publisher have made every effort to ensure the accuracy and completeness of information contained in this book, we assume no responsibility for errors, inaccuracies, omissions, or any inconsistency herein. Any slights of people, places, or organizations are unintentional.

For the People of Westborough,
Whose Passion for History
Seemingly Knows No Bounds

Contents

Preface ix

Acknowledgements xiii

Introduction 1

Westborough in Colonial Days 3

The Town Canon 5

Boycott of British Goods 9

Taverns 15

Tory Protesters 20

The Structure of Government and the Continental Congress 22

Increasing Tensions 26

What Were Militia Training Days? 30

Westborough's Militia 34

March to Worcester 36

Rev. Ebenezer Parkman 42

The British Point of View 45

Westborough's Move Towards Independence 49

The Declaration of Independence 51

Epilogue: How is Today Different? 54

    Town Meetings 54

    Farms 57

    Boycotts 59

Taverns.. **61**

Revolution... **62**

Community Celebrations **64**

Sources... **66**

Preface

This book came out of research I conducted while preparing an exhibit for the "1774 Westborough Militia Training Day" held in Westborough, MA at the Veteran's Freedom Park on October 14, 2017 as part of the town's 300ᵗʰ anniversary celebration. The goal for the exhibit was to use historical documents discovered in the Town Clerk's vault during the renovation of Westborough's Town Hall in 2013 to tell the story of Westborough's preparation and participation in the march to Worcester to close the Worcester County courts on September 6, 1774. Naturally, I had more to tell about the story than could fit on a series of exhibit panels, so I decided to create an "exhibition catalog" where I could go into more depth for people who were interested in the topic. The result is this book.

Like many Americans, I became obsessed with the American Revolution during our country's Bicentennial in 1976 and since then have carried a latent interest in colonial America. But I did not have direct connection to this history or to the places where these events took place at the time, because I grew up in Chicago, and whenever my family traveled on vacation, we always headed west. My exposure to Boston was mostly confined to PBS shows produced by WGBH, more specifically *Zoom*. New England seemed so distant to my young mind that ever seeing it in person was the equivalent of traveling to Europe. The fact that I settled with my wife and two daughters in Westborough—an idyllic small New England town in the heart of Massachusetts—continues to astonish me.

My interest in colonial America eventually became manifest when I decided to research and write two books on early American crime. While my exploration of this topic occasionally intersected with events of the American Revolution, it never answered a burning question of mine: what incentive prompted common people to unite around the cause of declaring independence from Great Britain—the mightiest empire in the world at the time—and then risk their lives to make it happen? We live in an age when Congress cannot seem to make even minor decisions due to the many factional interests that currently make up this legislative body. Yet during an age when communication was much slower than it is today, the American people became convinced of the need to separate from England and rallied around the idea of forging a new political identity. How did those who led this uprising persuade so many to join them?

The Rebellion Begins works towards answering these questions by looking closely at historical documents from the small town of Westborough, Massachusetts. These documents do not tell the town's whole story, because many of the records have been lost over time. But when the extant ones are put together and looked at in the context of broader histories of the American Revolution, an interesting picture begins to emerge. The people of Westborough quickly saw the direction in which Great Britain was taking them, and they did not like it. They signed on to early and decisive action to stop England from potentially infringing on their way of life.

Our notion of revolution usually involves people becoming fed up with deteriorating social conditions, rising up against the tyrannical oppressors imposing those conditions on them, and putting in place an entirely different system of government. Think the French Revolution, the Russian Revolution, or the Chinese Revolutions. The American Revolution certainly had elements similar to all these others, but in many ways, it is unique. After all, colonial America was the product of Great Britain, which itself had already gone through radical political change with the Glorious Revolution in 1688, when the Crown's authority was no longer bestowed by God but by Parliament. A close look at how Westborough participated in the events leading up to the American Revolution shows how different this revolution was from other major revolutions.

When we think about important social and political movements, it is perhaps natural to turn our attention to the people who seemed to lead those movements and consider them the heroes, but this case study of Westborough shows that the consent for rebellion during the American Revolution came from the people. Yes, we can identify leaders on many political levels who had an important hand in organizing revolt, but the American Revolution was truly a grass-roots effort. The leaders did not have to convince the people to rebel; the people chose to rebel, and the leaders helped facilitate their wishes.

People we read about in history occupy a special place that seems far removed from our daily lives. We can easily forget that they are much like you and me and simply reacted to the events and circumstances that were before them. While we sometimes are in awe at what they accomplished, we do not know how we would have reacted had we been in similar situations. At the same time, we sometimes read history and fall into the trap of believing that what happened then is much like what is happening now, that nothing has changed. But in embracing this circular conception of history, we lose the nuances that make history so fascinating and risk missing the lessons that history can teach us about the present and about the long road that has brought us to this point.

Many elements of the American Revolution remain with us today, although in different forms and with different agendas. As you read *The Rebellion Begins*, think about how you would have reacted had you faced similar situations, but also note how the time and place in which they happened was unique. The Epilogue will be a space to explore the connection between the themes of Westborough's history that appear in this book with some familiar early twenty-first century experiences. It will also be a place to think more about your own personal role in America's continuing revolutionary experiment.

Acknowledgements

Writing a book about Westborough and its role in starting the American Revolution was the furthest thing from my mind until I was invited as the Local History Librarian to sit in on a planning session for a militia day sponsored by the Westborough Rotary Club. I was charged with leading efforts to create an exhibit to provide people with context for what was happening out on the field during the event, and with this task, this book was born. So at the top of my list of people to thank is the Militia Day Committee: Ken Ferrera, Bill Gundling, Bill Linane, Hazel Nourse, Don Shapleigh, Ed Turner, and John Walden. Earl Storey and Paul Reilly supported our group by consulting with us on preparing the grounds for the event. Jim O'Connor, the committee chair, receives special thanks for his enthusiasm for the project and for keeping us all motivated and focused on our assignments. Leslie Leslie designed, edited, and contributed content to the exhibit panels, and without her help the exhibit never would have looked as professional as it did. Gary Gregory and I worked together on the educational aspects of the project, and his guidance was instrumental in shaping the entire project. Without all of these people, this book never would have happened.

I enjoyed working with the Militia Day Committee so much that I ended up joining the Westborough Rotary Club. The club's members are the nicest and most energetic group of people you will ever meet, and special thanks goes out to them and to the Presidents who presided over the club during our planning process, Gerry Gross and Shelby Marshall.

Ross W. Beales, Jr., Professor Emeritus of History at the College of the Holy Cross, generously shared both his knowledge and transcriptions of Rev. Ebenezer Parkman's *Diary* with me. Writing this book would have been much more time-consuming—and the book less comprehensive—without his assistance. Wendy Mickel, Westborough's Town Clerk, was enormously helpful in giving me access to important town records. And Kristina Allen freely shared her knowledge of this book's topic with me, not least through her seminal book on Westborough history, *On the Beaten Path*.

I have enjoyed every minute of my job as the Local History Librarian, and much of the credit for that goes to Maureen Ambrosino, the Westborough Public Library staff, and the Library Board of Trustees. They have all supported me in this project, and I appreciate the freedom they give me in growing the local history program at our library. Other institutions critical to the success of writing this book include the Westborough Historical Society, the Westborough Historical Commission, the American Antiquarian Society, the Digital Commonwealth, and the Boston Public Library.

Special thanks go to Luanne Crosby, who agreed to edit my manuscript after I decided to take a chance to secure "the best" editor and asked her. She and her partner, R. Christopher Noonan, along with Gary Gregory and his wife Angela Gregory, have become my biggest history cheerleaders and motivate me to keep pushing the limits of my historical knowledge of Westborough. My longtime friend David Syring stepped in and gave me valuable last-minute advice on the direction of this book, which I believe is much stronger as a result of his efforts.

And finally, as always, I thank my wife, Martha Heller, and my two daughters, Maddy Vaver and Audrey Vaver. Writing a book is an intense experience and requires sacrifices that impact the entire household. My family had to put up with delayed dinners, so that I could write just one more paragraph, and with my distractions during conversation as my brain worked on figuring out how the book should be structured. There is no way for me to express both my love for them and my appreciation of their support for my projects.

Introduction

"The Revolution was in the Minds of the People . . . before a drop of blood was drawn at Lexington."

—John Adams, Letter to Thomas Jefferson, 24 August 1815.

The fall of 1774 saw the Westborough militia stepping up its training in order to march to Worcester to shut down the Worcester County courts, now operating under the Intolerable Acts. Word had spread that General Thomas Gage was sending armed British soldiers into western Massachusetts to protect the courts and to enforce these new laws that stripped away civic rights enjoyed by Massachusetts citizens, including their ability to select their own government representatives and to hold their own town meetings. Westborough, along with other surrounding towns, began preparing for the possible confrontation.

Most people think April 19, 1775 marks the beginning of the American Revolution. The truth is, when the British marched into Lexington on that day, they were attempting to take back a colony that was no longer under their control. With the exception of Boston and Salem, by the fall of 1774 the people of Massachusetts had already completed their break from British rule, and Westborough was at the forefront of this dramatic change.

Colonial Americans were concerned with restraint of governmental power, protection from abuses of that power, and the security of their lives, liberty, and property. They were willing to fight to preserve their way of life, especially now that the British appeared to be progressively rolling back their freedoms. *The Rebellion Begins* is the story of how the people of Westborough sought to protect these values and, in so doing, rose up against the mighty British Empire and helped start the American Revolution.

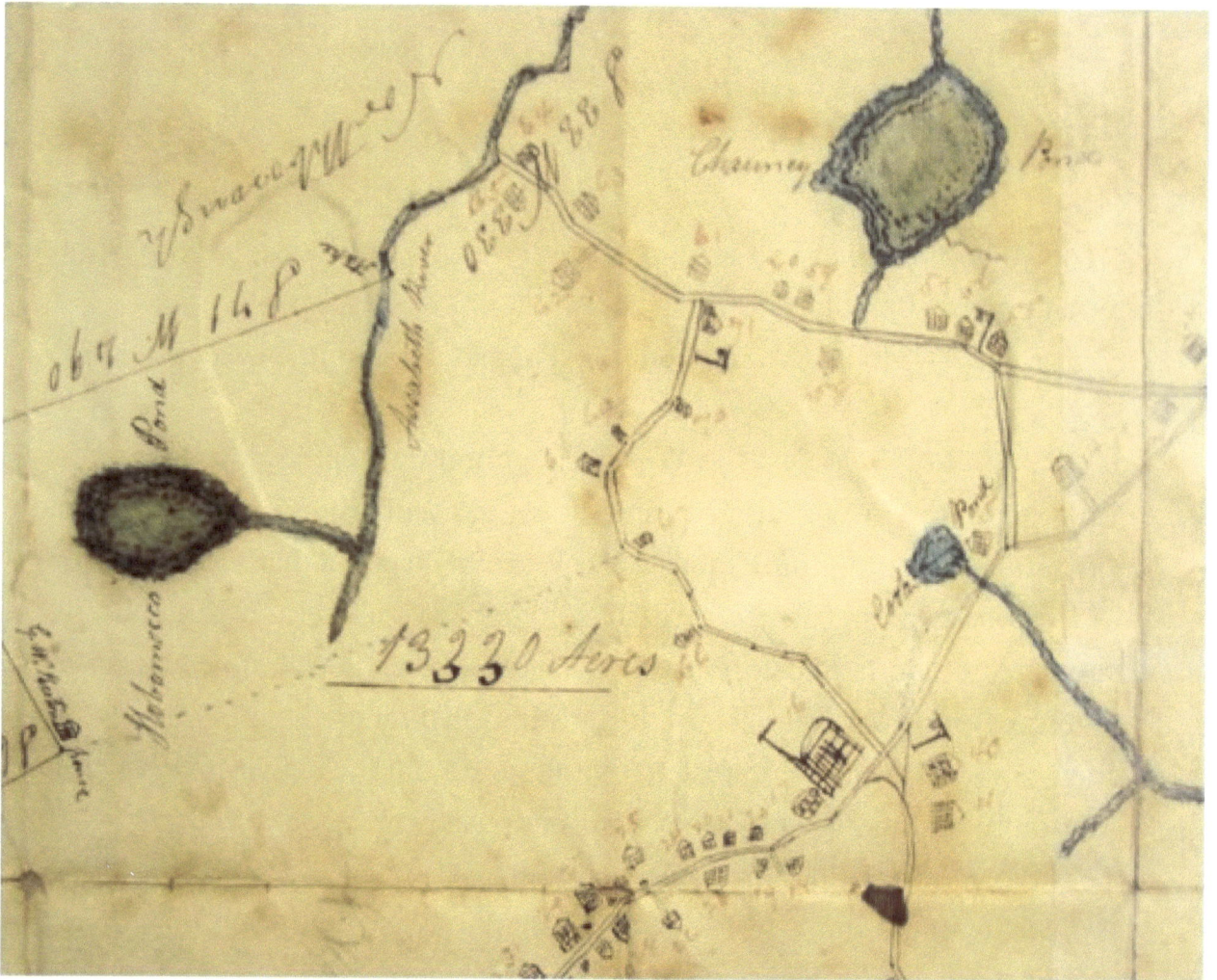

Map of Westborough, 1795 – Nathan Fisher
(Westborough Historical Society)

Westborough in Colonial Days

Westborough in 1774 was a typical New England town. It had a Congregational Church, a few taverns, artisan shops, and six school "squadrons." Most of its inhabitants were middle class and owned modest farms of roughly 50 to 100 acres. Typical crops for New England included flax for making fiber, Indian corn to feed people and livestock, beans, squash, potatoes, and apples for cider. Livestock generally included horses, oxen, cows, sheep, pigs, and chickens. While men tended the fields and livestock, women processed the farm's production by cooking, preserving, spinning, weaving, and sewing. The people were hard-working and spent most of their time with their animals or families, except for occasions when they gathered in town to worship at the church, drink and talk politics at the tavern, or drill for the militia.

Just like other New England towns, every March the constable for Westborough posted a warrant, or agenda, for a town meeting, and people gathered at the meetinghouse to elect officers and conduct town business for the year. More town meetings could be called throughout the year to take care of any pressing business that arose. These open forums trained the population to problem-solve within a large group in an orderly way and taught them the value of democratically deciding how they wanted to live their lives together. In sum, the people of Westborough had something to protect and fight for when they thought their rights and way of life were being threatened or taken away.

Rev. Ebenezer Parkman, Westborough's first minister, a pen and ink sketch by
a boy from memory (probably not an accurate likeness).
(Westborough Public Library)

The Town Canon

"The Tea that bainful weed is arrived."
—Abigail Adams, Letter to Mercy Otis Warren, 5 December 1773

Abigail Adams was referring to three East India Company ships that arrived in Boston from England. They were loaded with tea that would be subject to a new three pence duty when it was unloaded onto the mainland. In protest, Samuel Adams's "Mohawks" boarded the ships on the night of December 16, 1773 and dumped the tea into Boston Harbor. As punishment, the British Parliament passed a bill on March 25, 1774, to close the port of Boston, a move that could drastically affect farmers by cutting off markets for their produce. This legislation was the first in a series of acts passed by Parliament aimed at punishing colonists for the Boston Tea Party. Parliament called the acts the "Coercive Acts" and colonists called them the "Intolerable Acts." In addition to passing these punishing acts, the British government installed a new governor for Massachusetts, General Thomas Gage.

When the Boston Port Act went into effect on June 1, Rev. Ebenezer Parkman of Westborough noted in his diary, "Now begins a New and peculiar *AEra*: for this Day the Act of Parliament called the *Boston Port Bill*, whereby the Harbour of *Boston* is shut up, takes Effect. May God be pleased to Sanctifie this His holy Dispensation of Providence to this whole People!"

After Westborough received a letter from Boston dated May 12, 1774, informing the town of the passage of the Boston Port Act and Britain's intention to close down Boston Harbor, it held a special Town Meeting on June 13, 1774. In addition to creating a Committee of Correspondence to communicate with other towns, Westborough voted to take more aggressive action:

BOSTON, *May* 12, 1774.

GENTLEMEN,

BY the laſt advices from London we learn that an Act has been paſſed by the Britiſh Parliament for blocking up the Harbour of Boſton, with a Fleet of Ships of War, and preventing the Entrance in, or Exportation of, all Sorts of Merchandize, on Penalty of Forfeiture of the Goods and the Veſſels which carry them : And not only the Goods and Veſſels are to be forfeited, but the very Wharfinger who ſhall aſſiſt in lading or diſcharging ſuch Goods or Merchandize, ſhall forfeit treble their Value, at their higheſt Price, together with his Cattle, Horſes, Carriages, Implements whatſoever, made Uſe of in lading or landing them.

And under theſe grievous and unheard of Impoſitions are we to remain till his Majeſty in Council ſhall be certified by the Governor or Lieutenant Governor, that a *full Obedience* is yielded to the *Laws* of a Britiſh Parliament, and the Revenue duly collected ; and alſo that the Eaſt-India Company have received full Satisfaction for their Teas, and the Revenue Officers, and others for their Sufferings, by their Endeavours to fix the Tea Duty upon us. And even then, the whole Port of *Boſton* with all its Wharves, Quays, &c. ſhall be under the abſolute Controul of his Majeſty, and no Article of Merchandize landed on or laded from any of them, but ſuch as he ſhall licence, on the Penalty aboveſaid.

By this Means, even in Caſe of the moſt abject Submiſſion, and unconditional Obedience, the private Property, in moſt of the Wharves which ſurround this great Town, is raviſhed from the rightful Owners, and rendered uſeleſs, to the utter Ruin of many worthy Citizens, in Revenge to the Patriotiſm of ſome, whom probably this Clauſe was inſerted to puniſh.

To this alarming Situation has the Machinations of our Enemies here and in Great-Britain reduced us : And as this is a Cauſe ſo intereſting to *all* America—A Cauſe which has been hitherto ſo nobly defended by ALL, we cannot entertain a Thought ſo diſhonorable to our Friends, that in this Criſis *we* ſhall be left to ſtruggle *alone*.

We are, Gentlemen,

Your Friends and Fellow Countrymen,

By Order of the Committee,

William Cooper Town Clerk

P. S. As it has been induſtriouſly and wickedly propagated that the patriotic Col. BARRE had become our Enemy, we can aſſure you that in a Speech on this Bill he expreſſed himſelf in theſe emphatic Terms, " *America is ſtamped upon every Loom and Anvil in Great-Britain.*" In plain Engliſh, let America diſcontinue its Trade, and the Britiſh Manufacturer muſt *emigrate* or *ſtarve*.

N. B. This Letter was written in Preſence of and with the Concurrence of the Committees of Correſpondence for the Towns of Dorcheſter, Roxbury, Newtown, Lexington, Brooklyn, Cambridge, Charleſtown and Lynn.

Letter from Boston – May 12, 1774
(Library of Congress)

Voted to bye a Field Peice a 4 Pounder and 4 Hundred wt of Ball

Voted to Chuse a Committee to bye the Said Field Peice and Ball and procure a Carriag

Voted to procure Ten Halfe Barrils of Powder 5 Hundred wt of Lead & Flints

Westborough's response to the closing of Boston Harbor was to arm itself, and it would start with the purchase of a canon.

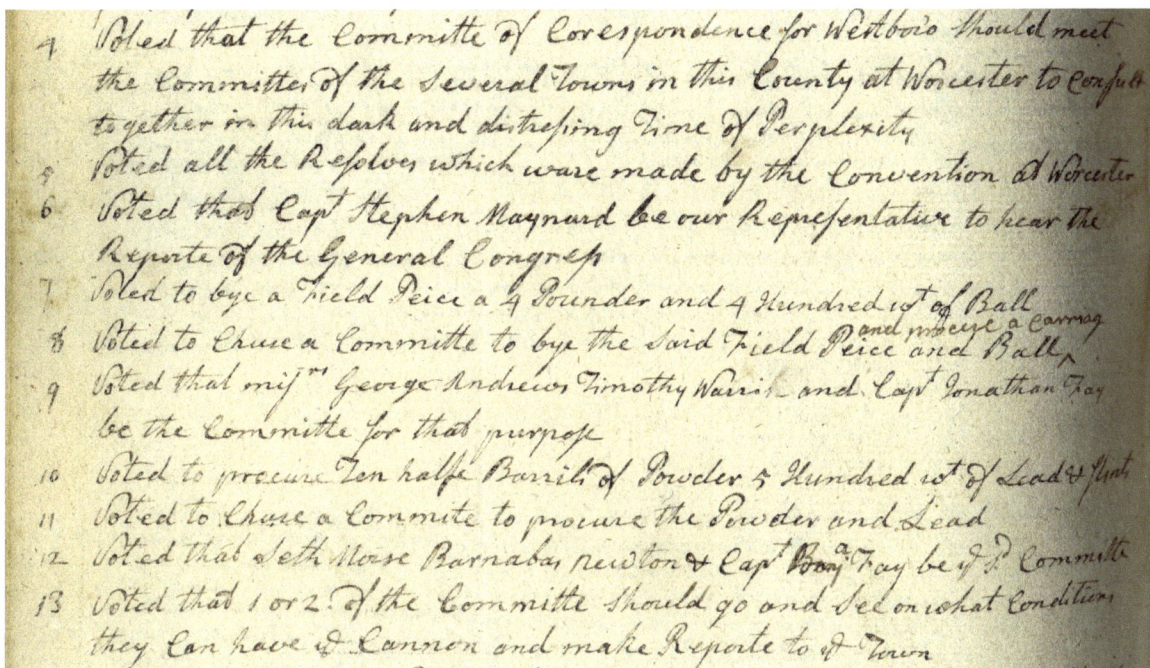

Detail from *Town Meeting Records*, June 13, 1774 – Vote to purchase a town canon
(Westborough Town Clerk's Office)

During the same meeting, Westborough voted to make Capt. Stephen Maynard Chief Commander over the various militia companies in town and urged anyone willing to enlist in the companies to do so as soon as possible. In addition, the town ordered each company to train and arm themselves and for anyone else to do the same. When calls went out in the fall for Massachusetts towns to arm themselves and to purchase one or more canons in order to defend themselves against possible British aggression, Westborough was already well prepared.

To mr Martin Pratt Constable you are hereby ordered to pay to nathan Fisher out of the Town money one Pound nine Shillings and Four pence to Satisfie him for all that he found and did to Fix and prepair our Cannon and his Receipt Shall be your discharge for so much by order of the Select-men   Jonª Bond Town Clerk

Westboro May 22ᵈ 1774

£ 1 - 9 - 4

Westborough
May ye 22   1775

Receiv'd of Mr Martin Pratt the Sum of one Pound nine Shilling & four pence of the town Money which was Due to me for work that is I did towards the Cannon in full
I say Rec'd by me Nathan Fisher

Order for payment and receipt to repair the town canon, May 22, 1775
(Digital Commonwealth/Westborough Public Library)

Boycott of British Goods

To counteract the passage of the Boston Port Act, the Boston Committee of Correspondence composed and circulated a "Solemn League and Covenant" for citizens to sign as a pledge not to consume any British goods after August 31. Such tactics not only served as a means of hitting the British hard in their pocketbook, but were also a way to create solidarity and force people to take sides in the conflict. On Monday, July 4, 1774, the town of Westborough met to hear how its own Committee of Correspondence would respond to the petition. Rev. Ebenezer Parkman read some of his own reflections on the matter to the group, but then ducked out of the meeting before the Committee presented its decisions. "*I did not care to meddle with it*," he noted in his diary, "for I conceived it was not *safe* for me to do it, Safe either *for me* or for *them*, especially by reason of the *Governors Proclamation*." Despite a decree by General Gage to arrest anyone who circulated or signed the petition, many Westborough residents took up the boycott after several weeks of debate.

In a sign of protest, people now started drinking coffee rather than tea, to the point where per capita coffee consumption in the United States increased more than seven times between 1770 and 1790—Americans have been coffee drinkers ever since. On July 27, 1774, Rev. Parkman, made a special note in his diary that during a visit to his house by Dr. James Hawes—a member of Westborough's Committee of Correspondence—he and his Wife "drink Chocolat (instead of Tea)," chocolate being another protest drink of choice, and he notes in later entries when visitors to his house drink coffee.

WE the Subscribers, Inhabitants of the Town of having taken into our serious Consideration, the precarious State of the LIBERTIES of NORTH-AMERICA, and more especially the present distressed Condition of our Sister Colony of the Massachusetts-Bay, embarrassed as it is by several Acts of the British Parliament, tending to the entire Subversion of their natural and Charter Rights; among which is the *Act for blocking up the Harbour of* BOSTON: And being fully sensible of our indispensible Duty to lay hold on every Means in our Power to preserve and recover the much injured Constitution of our Country; and conscious at the same Time of no Alternative between the Horrors of Slavery, or the Carnage and Desolation of a civil War, but a Suspension of all commercial Intercourse with the Island of Great-Britain, DO, in the Presence of GOD, solemnly and in good Faith, covenant and engage with each other.

1. That from henceforth we will suspend all commercial Intercourse with the said Island of Great-Britain, until the Parliament shall cease to enact Laws imposing Taxes upon the Colonies, without their Consent, or until the pretended Right of Taxing is dropped. And

2. That there may be less Temptation to others to continue in the said now dangerous Commerce; and in order to promote Industry, Oeconomy, Arts and Manufactures among ourselves, which are of the last Importance to the Welfare and Well-being of a Community; we do, in like Manner, solemnly covenant, that we will not buy, purchase or consume, or suffer any Person, by, or under us, to purchase, nor will we use in our Families in any Manner whatever, any Goods, Wares or Merchandise which shall arrive in America from Great-Britain aforesaid, from and after the last Day of August next ensuing (except only such Articles as shall be judged absolutely necessary by the Majority of the Signers hereof;--and as much as in us lies, to prevent our being interrupted and defeated in this only peaceable Measure entered into for the Recovery and Preservation of our Rights, and the Rights of our Brethren in our Sister Colonies, We argree to break of all Trade and Commerce, with all Persons, who prefering their private Interest to the Salvation of their now almost perishing Country, as shall still continue to import Goods from Great-Britain, or shall purchase of those who import after the said last Day of August, until the aforesaid pretended Right of Taxing the Colonies shall be given up or dropped.

3. As a Refusal to come into any Agreement which promises Deliverance of our Country from the Calamities it now feels, and which, like a Torrent, are rushing upon it with increasing Violence, must, in our Opinion, evidence a Disposition enemical to, or criminally negligent of the common Safety :---It is agreed, that all such ought to be considered, and shall by us be esteemed, as Encouragers of contumacious Importers.

Lastly, We hereby further engage, that we will use every Method in our Power, to encourage and promote the Production of Manufactures among ourselves, that this Covenant and Engagement may be as little detrimental to ourselves and Fellow Countrymen as possible.

Petition to boycott British goods, 1774
(Library of Congress)

The British Parliament continued its punishment for the Boston Tea Party by passing the Massachusetts Government Act. Under this act, the people of Massachusetts could still elect town officers, but any local decisions had to be approved by the governor. They could vote for House representatives, but this body no longer controlled the actions of government officials (judges, justices of the peace, sheriffs, etc.) or had influence over the governor and his councilors. And finally, town meetings could no longer take place without the consent of the governor and could only follow a pre-approved agenda in an attempt to limit organized dissent. This move not only disenfranchised the citizens of the colony, but in the eyes of the people, directly violated the 1691 charter for Massachusetts, which they considered a binding contract between them and Great Britain.

Eighteenth-century foil-lined tea case with lock
(Westborough Historical Society)

Up until 1774, most rebellious activity centered in Boston, but in the summer of that year the scene of conflict suddenly shifted to the western countryside. If farmers were divided in their opinion over dumping tea into Boston Harbor, they could all agree that the Massachusetts Government Act was a direct threat to their liberty and well-being. The Town of Westborough had developed a protectionist stance towards its liberties well before this current crisis. Back in January 1773, Boston circulated a pamphlet outlining increased British aggression toward the colony and asked if Massachusetts towns wanted to open up communication to coordinate resistance. A committee of seven in Westborough was convened to consider the matter, and they responded,

> Under ye present critical and alaruming Situation of our publick affairs There is a loud call to every one to awake from Security & in Earnest strive to secure his Liberty, lest he politically perish . . . For no Dought ware tyranny is Exercised, Opposition becomes a duty. As our fathers could, so can we plead our Loyalty; we have been, and now are, Ready to spill our Dearest blood in Defence of our King, Religion & Constitutional Laws. We cannot but look upon it a hard Trial, yea greater than we can bear, if we cannot Give full proof of our Loyalty Otherwise than by sacrificing those Rights & Liberties which we prize beyond life itself.

The letter was signed by Phineas Hardy (chair), Capt. Benjamin Fay, Daniel Forbes, Hananiah Parker, Ebenezer Maynard, Abijah Gale, and Dr. James Hawes.

Over the summer of 1774, people in town regularly visited Rev. Parkman in an attempt to get him to sign the Covenant to boycott British goods, or at least learn his position towards the petition. Each time, Parkman put them off by saying that he needed more time to consider the matter. On August 1, the town held yet another meeting to consider the boycott, and at this meeting Parkman's son, Breck, signed the Covenant. Rev. Parkman himself showed up to the meeting with "a paper fit to be subscribed and read it to a Number of persons," but the people effectively ignored him and never asked him to read it aloud to the group.

Breck Parkman, son of Rev. Ebenezer Parkman
(Westborough Public Library)

Finally, on August 29, Rev. Parkman was forced to show his hand: "Mr. *Morse* came here in the Morning, full of Earnestness, and lays before me the great Disquietment in Town by Reason of my not Signing something or other, if it were a Draught of my own etc. Rather than have such a Hubbub and uproar, I Conceived it to be my duty to Sign what I carryed to the meeting House on the 1st instant." Unfortunately, we do not know the content of what Rev. Parkman eventually signed, but it was certainly a more conservative stance toward the boycott than what was contained in the Covenant. Later that day, Parkman attended Capt. Seth Morse's militia training exercises, prayed with the company, and then returned home.

The Able Doctor, or America Swallowing the Bitter Draught, 1774. "Cartoon shows Lord North, with the 'Boston Port Bill' extending from a pocket, forcing tea (the Intolerable Acts) down the throat of a partially draped Native female figure representing 'America' whose arms are restrained by Lord Mansfield, while Lord Sandwich, a notorious womanizer, restrains her feet and peeks up her skirt. Britannia, standing behind 'America,' turns away and shields her face with her left hand."
(Digital Commonwealth/Boston Public Library)

Taverns

People frequently gathered in taverns to socialize in colonial New England. Worcester County had one tavern for every forty to fifty adult males during the colonial period, and each tavern contained between sixteen to forty-four chairs. The main drink of choice was cider, but people also drank grain or potato whiskey, maple or cherry-flavored rum, and peach brandy. Two taverns in Westborough served as focal points for the town's revolutionary activity, the Gale Tavern and the Blue Anchor Tavern.

Amsden-Gale Tavern, 250 East Main Street, ca. 1890
(Westborough Public Library)

In 1719, two years after the founding of Westborough, Jacob Amsden built a tavern at 250 East Main Street. His aristocratic background drew royal magistrates, officers, and government officials traveling between Boston and Worcester to his establishment. But under the leadership of Abijah Gale, who took over the tavern in 1771, the establishment's clientele shifted away from royalists to rebels. In fact, Gale was one of the signers of Westborough's letter supporting coordinated resistance to British tyranny in January 1773. The Gale Tavern eventually became the social center for the town militia after they completed their training in a nearby field and it served as their meeting point before they marched off to action during the American Revolution. George Washington stopped at the Gale Tavern on July 2, 1776 as he made his way to Cambridge to take command of the American forces. The tavern closed in the early 1800's.

Blue Anchor Tavern, 108 West Main Street, 1923
(Westborough Public Library)

The Blue Anchor Tavern was another center of political activity for Westborough during the years leading up to the American Revolution: Westborough's response to Boston's January 1773 call to coordinate communication among Massachusetts towns was written and signed here; the Committee of Correspondence met at the tavern to craft complaints against British attempts to limit the rights of Westborough townspeople in 1774; and the Selectmen would meet in secret with the Committee of Correspondence at the Blue Anchor. The tavern also served as a stopping point for troops marching from Boston to southern New England during the Revolutionary War. In 1820, the building was reportedly moved from the current high school property to 108 West Main Street, where it still stands today.

The House of Dr. James Hawes, 114 East Main Street (the former "Plaster House"), ca. 1890. Dr. Hawes served on Westborough's Committee of Correspondence (Westborough Public Library)

Townspeople who served on Westborough's Committees of Correspondence

- **Lieut. Joseph Baker** - Also known as the "Squire." In 1773, he invited Breck Parkman and others to his home on 115 W. Main Street to form Westborough's first cooperative library society. He served as a Selectman in 1768 and was named Captain of Artillery in July 1774.
- **Jonathan Bond** - Fought in the French and Indian War and served as a Deacon in the Congregational Church. He was a Selectman, the Town Clerk (in 1774), and a Representative to the General Court.
- **Thomas Bond** - The son of Jonathan, he served as the First Lieutenant of the militia unit under Capt. Edward Brigham.
- **Capt. Benjamin Fay** - Said to have commanded companies in the French and Indian War. He served many years as a Selectman, including in 1774, and as Town Treasurer. His house was on 38 Nourse St.
- **Daniel Forbes** - Served as a Representative in 1777.
- **Abijah Gale** - Owned the Gale Tavern at 250 E. Main St. He served as Town Constable, a school committee member, the first member of the Overseers of the Poor, highway surveyor, and chair of the Selectmen from 1778 to 1780.
- **Phineas Hardy** - Served as the Chair of the Committee of Correspondence and was a Selectman.
- **Joseph Harrington** - Served as a Selectman over many years starting in 1778. He lived at 116 Ruggles St.
- **Dr. James Hawes** - Lived at 114 E. Main St. (The former "Plaster House" near the corner of Lyman Street). He was the first town physician and served as a Selectmen, Town Clerk, and Town Constable. He dispensed his own medicine and extracted teeth. He also served as the Justice of the Peace and held minor court cases in his home, at the Blue Anchor Tavern, or at the Gale Tavern. He rented out horses and rooms in his house and was one of the founders of the Baptist Church.
- **Ebenezer Maynard** - Elected Town Treasurer in 1745 at the age of 29 and served as a Selectman for many years, including 1774.
- **Capt. Stephen Maynard** - Served as Selectman and as a Representative from 1768-1777 and from 1785-1789.
- **Hananiah Parker** - Served as a Representative in 1782.

Large etched flip glass with wooden "toddy stick"
(Westborough Historical Society)

Tory Protesters

People loyal to the Crown were usually called "Tories," and in rural Massachusetts they tended to be members of the upper class and enjoyed social and political power while the colony still fell under British control. At a Worcester town meeting on May 16, 1774, a group of elite citizens with notable sympathies with the British were outnumbered and overruled by the majority of the people when deciding on orders to give to the town's representative to the General Court. In the end, the group at town meeting ordered their representative to denounce the closure of the Boston port, to reject issuing compensation for the tea that was dumped into Boston Harbor, and to support the creation of a Continental Congress.

Dissatisfied with the result, the Tories tried to call a special meeting to reconsider the previous vote. When they were again outvoted, they drafted a dissent to be entered into the town records, but the patriots blocked even this action. Clark Chandler, the town clerk, nonetheless entered the dissent into the books. Their dissent became known as the Tory "Protest," and their petition was printed and circulated in the Boston newspapers, along with a list of the names of the "Worcester Protesters."

Worcefter Protefters.

CAptain Daniel Ward,
John Walker, half pay Officer.
Nathaniel Adams,
William Campbell, Scotch Trader.
Samuel Moor, Innholder.
Lieut. John Mower,
Jofeph Blair,
Capt. Micah Johnfon,
Sergt. Edmund Heard, Baker.
Thomas Baird,
Capt. Samuel Mower,
Lieut. Samuel Bridge, Barber.
Deacon Jacob Chamberlain,
Andrew Duncan, Scotch Trader.
Capt. James Goodwin,
Clark Chandler, Trader. Son to Judge Chandler.
Capt. Ifrael Jenifon, Waggoner.
Nathan Patch,
Samuel Mower, jun.
Ifaac Moor,
Jofhua Johnfon, Deputy Sheriff.
John Chandler, Judge of Probate.
Gardner Chandler, Sheriff.
James Putnam, Barrifter.
Daniel Boyden,
Capt. John Curtis, Innholder.
Thomas Baird,
James Hart,
Capt. Elifha Smith, Waggoner.
Capt. Tyrus Rice,
Doct. Nahum Willard,
Rufus Chandler, Lawer.
Capt. Palmer Goulding, Shoemaker, Tanner,
(and Malfter.
Adam Walker, Blackfmith.
David Moor, Deputy Sheriff.
James Hart, jun.
Cornelius Stowell, Weaver and Dyer.
Jonathan Phillips,
Capt. Samuel Brooks, Shoe Maker.
Ifaac Willard, Blackfmith.
Jacob Stevens,
Ifrael Stevens,
Jofeph Clark,
Ifaac Barnard,
William Pain, Druggift.
Thadeus Chamberlain,
Enfign John Chamberlain,
William Curtis,
Abel Stowell, Clock-maker.
Daniel Goulding, Shoe-maker.
William Chandler, a Boy.

List of Worcester Protesters
(Digital Commonwealth/Westborough Public Library)

The Structure of Government and the Continental Congress

The general structure of Massachusetts government during colonial times was similar to ours today. The main ruling body was the General Court, which was composed of the House of Representatives and the Council, both of which were essentially elected by the people and functioned as the lower and upper bodies of the legislature, despite its misleading name. The General Court could oversee the distribution of the province's lands, levy taxes, and enact laws. But by 1774, the General Court did not exercise great power because most land had already been distributed, there were few taxes because there were few services, and laws could be challenged by other government entities. At the local level, town meetings functioned like the General Court in that they could enact laws, but these meetings were mostly concerned with administrative affairs. Selectmen were charged with carrying out most of the tasks set out by Town Meeting.

The Governor oversaw and appointed members of the executive branch of the government, which included the Lieutenant Governor, Secretary, Treasurer, and other lesser officials. This branch possessed even less power than the General Court, since its main function was to execute laws and call upon the military if necessary.

The courts, the third branch of colonial government, basically served as a link between the provincial government and the local communities. Each county had a Court of General Sessions, which essentially oversaw the mechanisms of local government, and an Inferior Court of Common Pleas, which handled all civil suits. Much like our system of government today, each branch had specific duties and each limited the power of the others, but because the courts had the power to fine, punish, or coerce individuals, they held the most power out of all three branches of government.

Tax Bill to the Town, June 17, 1774 (signed by Samuel Adams before "Clerk")
(Digital Commonwealth/Westborough Public Library)

On June 17, 1774, after the passage of the Intolerable Acts, the House of Representatives met in Salem and enlisted the help of other colonies to resist British action. The Representatives pointed out that if the British government could strip away the charter and the democratic rights of citizens in Massachusetts, then it could do so in any other colony as well. The assembly called for a meeting of Committees from the various colonies to discuss the situation and proposed a gathering in Philadelphia on September 1. The General Court elected delegates to this planned Continental Congress and authorized payment of £500 to the delegates to offset their expenses. Not surprisingly, Governor Gage vetoed these actions.

Ignoring the veto, Samuel Adams sent out an appeal in the form of a Tax Bill to the towns of Massachusetts to share in the costs for sending delegates to Philadelphia. Westborough's portion came to £1 9*s.* 1*d.*, which the town promptly paid.

Samuel Adams, by John Singleton Copley, ca. 1772
(Museum of Fine Arts, Boston)

Increasing Tensions

The Court of Common Pleas was the more powerful of the two courts in Worcester, since it could make or break a person with its decisions regarding the collection and payment of debts. In 1773 and 1774, the Worcester Court of Common Pleas saw a 50% spike in debt cases. Not only did this increase create economic anxiety throughout the region—losing one's farm meant losing one's freedom, a farmer's worst fear—but people began to think that the increase was a move by elite forces to grab power and property from the more common folk.

The Massachusetts Government Act was set to take effect on August 1, and the farmers in western Massachusetts were not happy with the fact that the three-member panel of county judges would no longer be approved by elected representatives but by the Crown-appointed Governor, nor with the restrictions imposed on town meetings. More and more, the people of Westborough were seeing the rights and freedoms that they had enjoyed for years disappearing. On July 1, 1774, Ebenezer Parkman noted that his son Breck had gone to a "Military Meeting" at Lt. Joseph Baker's and then laments:

> All those Expressions in the public News Papers which are further irritating to Authority are my continual Grief, but I would willingly, heartily, promote what ever is lawful, constitutional and consistent with Wisdom and prudence under our unhappy Circumstances, and that is our Duty under our Christian Obligations to undertake for our Relief, and for the Restoration of our privileges and Liberties, that we may again enjoy under God our wonted Peace and Harmony with Great Britain.

On July 26, those attending a town meeting in Boston voted to send a letter to Westborough and other towns in Massachusetts through their

Committee of Correspondence. The letter outlines three areas of concern: 1) the acts of Parliament that consolidate power in the hands of British authorities; 2) recent corruption on the part of Peter Oliver—the Chief Justice of the Superior Court—in accepting extra overseas payments from the government; and 3) a strengthening military presence in the city. These actions by the British government, the letter predicts, "will bring on a most important and decisive trial." The letter goes on to thank the towns in Massachusetts for their past support and asks them to continue their aid in the future. Tensions across all of Massachusetts were beginning to mount.

The Town of Boston in New England and Brittish Ships of War Landing Their Troops!, 1768
(Digital Commonwealth/Boston Public Library)

AT a meeting of the freeholders and other inhabitants of the town of Boston, duly qualified and legally warned, in public town meeting, assembled at Faneuil-hall, on Tuesday the 26th day of July, Anno Domini 1774, at 10 o'clock forenoon.

VOTED, THAT a printed copy of the following letter to our brethren in the several towns and districts in the province be forthwith signed by the Town-Clerk, and transmitted by the Committee of Correspondence in the name and behalf of this town.

Attest.

William Cooper Town Clerk

FRIENDS and BRETHREN,

OUR public calamities have for a series of years been increasing both in number and weight. We have endeavoured under all our public misfortunes to conduct as good citizens in a COMMON CAUSE. Being stationed by providence in the front rank of the conflict, it hath been our aim to behave with vigilance, activity and firmness. To warn our brethren of approaching danger, to encounter with becoming spirit the trials of our patience, hath been our aim and our duty. Our friends and generous countrymen have given us reason to think we have not altogether failed in our honest endeavors in the way of this duty.

Two acts of parliament, altering the course of justice, and annihilating our once free constitution of government, are every day expected.

When we consider the conduct of our late worthy house of representatives, relative to our superior court Judges, and their impeachment of the Honorable Peter Oliver, Esq; for his accepting a salary from the crown in his office of Chief Justice; and when we consider the uniform spirit and conduct of the several Grand Jurors through the province, touching the same grievance, since that impeachment ; we cannot but suppose the aforementioned acts will bring on a most important and decisive trial.

You, gentlemen, our friends, countrymen and benefactors, may possibly look towards us at this great crisis. We trust that we shall not be left of Heaven to do any thing derogatory to our common liberties, unworthy the fame of our ancestors, or inconsistent with our former professions and conduct.

Though surrounded with a large body of armed men (who, having the sword, have also our blood in their hands) we are yet undaunted ; we trust in the GOD of our fathers, and we feel the animating support of a good cause ; but while suffering, a DOUBLE weight of oppression, and exasperated by a military camp in the very bowels of our town, our minds are not more in a temper to DELIBERATE, than our bodies in a situation to MOVE, as the perils and exigencies of the times may probably demand.

To you, gentlemen, our brethren and dear companions *in the cause of GOD and our country,* we apply ; from you we have *received that countenance and aid,* which have strengthened our hands, *and that bounty which hath occasioned smiles on the face of distress :* To you, therefore, we look for that *wisdom, advice* and EXAMPLE, which, giving strength to our understanding, and vigor to our actions, shall, with the blessing of GOD, save us from destruction.

Looking up to Heaven, and, under divine direction, to our brethren in the country and on the continent, for aid and support, and with earnest prayers for a happy issue out of our great troubles, We are, Your

FRIENDS and BRETHREN,

The INHABITANTS of BOSTON.

By order of the Town,

William Cooper Town Clerk

Letter from Inhabitants of Boston, July 26, 1774
(Digital Commonwealth/Westborough Public Library)

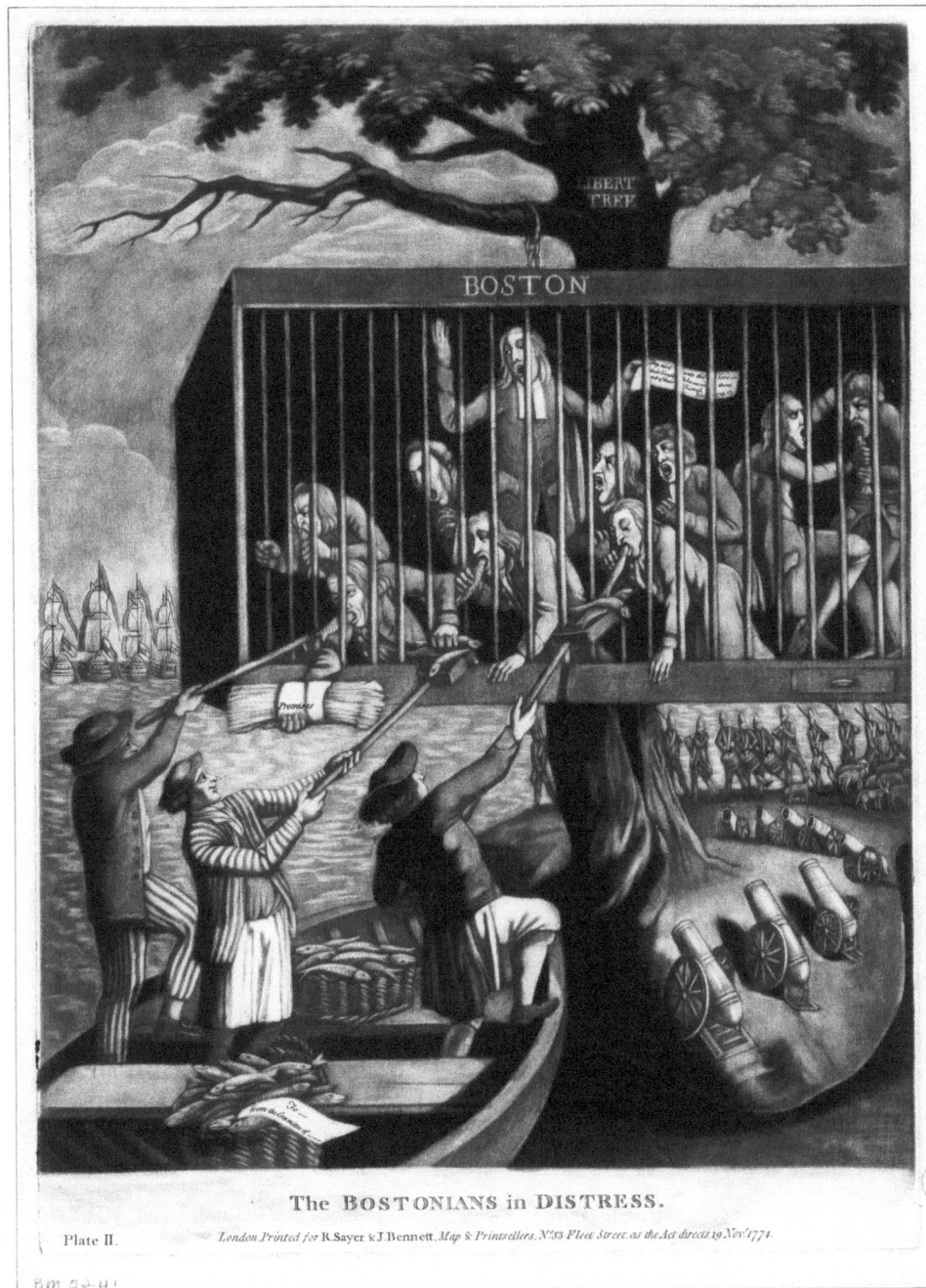

The Bostonians in Distress by Philip Dawe, November 19, 1774 – "The print shows
ten Bostonians in a huge cage suspended from the Liberty Tree. British seamen
hand them fish while cannons, ships and soldiers surround them in the background.
This was published at the time Boston had been closed by the Port of Boston Bill in
retaliation for the Boston Tea Party"
(Digital Commonwealth/Boston Public Library)

What Were Militia Training Days?

Militia Training Days go back to the very beginning of the colony. In the absence of professional soldiers, early New Englanders had to learn how to defend themselves from attacks by Native Americans, so they organized themselves into militia units and conducted training exercises. These militia units were organized by Company and were run by a Captain, who was assisted by a Lieutenant.

Times for training were set by law, and because the training cut into the occupations and well-being of the people who participated, their frequency changed from once a week, in the early days of the colony, to two small training days and one big training day every year by about 1750. Militia days were great social events and involved everyone in the community. While the men drilled and drank on the field, women and children gathered to watch the proceedings and socialize. Booths lined the grounds with food and other items to sell, gingerbread being a particular favorite.

Eighteenth-century French-made flintlock musket
(Westborough Historical Society)

Most militia training days consisted of a formal set of practices. After roll call, each man ceremoniously passed his musket to the officer for inspection to make sure it was clean and then it was handed back. Cartridge boxes were also examined, and knapsacks were put on the ground and opened for evaluation. The inspector then delivered an address of criticism or praise. At noon, the men were called into formation, and the colonel would inspect the lines. The regiments would then march for review, and the chaplain would give a prayer—a practice that was unique to New England. After all the formality, everyone scattered to dine and feast. The significance of training days was not just in drilling the soldier, but also in the patriotism and solidarity that they created.

In Westborough, Rev. Ebenezer Parkman would often lead prayer with the troops and officers. In his diary, Parkman described a particularly large militia training day that was held on October 3, 1739:

> The Regiment Under the Command of Colonel William Ward consisting of 11 Companys, muster'd and perform'd the Exercises proper on That Occasion. . . . We march'd with the Field Officers in Viewing the Regiment as the Battalion were in array, the Officers in their Places, and performing the Standing Salute. Mr. Dorr pray'd. We were entertain'd by the Field Officers. It was worthy of Notice that the Exercises were perform'd so well, considering their Newness, that there was so little hurt Done, and that there was So little intemperance, Rabblement and Riot. N.B. The Regiment under Colonel Chandler muster'd the same Day.

Even though Parkman was impressed by the conduct of the soldiers in 1739, he noted some rebellion among the ranks at a militia training day held on June 12, 1744:

> Captain Maynard's Training. Great Ruffle and Contests in the Breasts and partly breaking forth in the Conduct and Conversations of many of the North side soldiers. . . . A great Favour that Colonel Nahum Ward and Colonel Williams came, and were present at Reading the Laws, Viewing arms etc. that the unruly might be rebuk'd and kept down. N.B. It had been said that a certain Man on the North side [promised?] a Gallon of Rum if they would rebell against Captain Maynard—and a man was ready (as it was conceived) to head them. Mr. Wheeler was thot to be the

first of these and Corporal Nathan Ball the other. But in Public and whenever I was present I saw no indecency for which I was greatly rejoic'd and that Captain Eager and Lieutenant Holloway din'd with us at Captain Maynards.

Training days took place at various locations in Westborough, including the corner of Lyman and Main Street on what was then the Forbush property and on Brigham's farm on Walker Street. They were big days with large gatherings. Training days in New England peaked during the 1820s, but died out by 1840, a trend that held true in Westborough.

**Lieut. Thomas Forbush House, near East Main and Lyman Street, ca. 1890,
built ca. 1720. The house burned down on June 29, 1895.
(Westborough Public Library)**

On August 27, 1774, a committee met in Boston and drew up a report that called for the people of Massachusetts to learn "the Military Art according to the Norfolk Plan . . . as necessary means to secure their Liberties against the designs of Enemies whether Foreign or Domestick." Westborough followed suit. As political tensions rose in Massachusetts during the second half of 1774, Westborough held an increasing number of training days. These militia days, which had mostly functioned as social events in previous years, became more serious as the men began training for the possibility of real battle.

Westborough's Militia

John Adams believed that one of the four cornerstones of New England society was its militias, along with towns, congregations, and schools. Westborough's militia was made up of men between the ages of sixteen and sixty—intergenerational participation was an important component of militia training days—and was formed soon after the town was founded. Officer positions conferred prestige on those who held them, so like most towns in western Massachusetts, Westborough's officers were also town leaders. Even though the elite tended to head New England militias, both rich and poor participated in the militia system, unlike in England, which wanted to keep arms out of the hands of the lower classes to remove the possibility of rebellion.

Captain Stephen Maynard—who was named Chief Commander over all of the militia companies in Westborough at the same meeting when the town voted to purchase a canon—had been a lieutenant in the King's army for 20 years and served in the French and Indian War. At the time he was named Chief Commander, he was the wealthiest man in town, owned over 500 acres of land (mostly on Milk Street), and had at least three slaves (a couple and their daughter). At one point he was also a selectman and served as the town's representative to the Massachusetts House of Representatives and the Provincial Congress. Maynard's prominence in town did not last throughout his life. He eventually moved to Vermont to escape collectors after falling into heavy debt and most likely died there. His house in Westborough burned down on December 10, 1891.

The Captain Stephen Maynard House
(American Antiquarian Society)

* * *

Townspeople who served as Militia Officers in 1774

- Lt. Joseph Baker
- Lt. Thomas Bond
- Capt. Edmund Brigham
- Capt. Stephen Maynard
- Capt. Seth Morse
- Lt. Moses Wheelock

March to Worcester

The controversial Massachusetts Government Act went into effect on August 1, 1774. In protest, angry citizens began to block the meetings of county courts, whose authority no longer came from their elected officials but from officials appointed by the British government. In Worcester, the newly constituted courts were set to convene on September 6 and 7 and rumors had spread that General Gage was going to deploy British troops from Boston to keep them from being shut down.

* * *

Only a week or two earlier, Worcester had called on the surrounding towns to make a "march to Worcester," which in a way served as a dry run for what would come later. On August 24 after a town meeting, Worcester patriots decided that Clark Chandler—the clerk who entered the protest of the Tories into Worcester's town records back in May—should be forced to strike the objections from the records. Under watch, Chandler dutifully took up his pen and crossed out the text. Not to stop there, the patriots came up with a plan to force the resignations of the three local counselors and decided first to target Timothy Paine. On Friday, August 26, 1774, riders from Worcester alerted surrounding towns—including Westborough, Leicester, Spencer, Shrewsbury, Grafton, and Sutton—to their plan. Farmers mustered and traveled to Worcester that night if they were too far away, while others left before dawn to ride into Worcester before daybreak. Even though Worcester had fewer than 350 adult males living in town at the time, a crowd of 1,500 to 3,000 people showed up at the Worcester Common that Saturday morning.

General Thomas Gage, by John Singleton Copley, ca. 1768
(Yale Centre For British Art - Yale University, New Haven)

Around 9 a.m. on August 27, the crowd gathered around Timothy Paine's house and forced him to write and sign a letter of resignation. But the crowd was not satisfied with this simple act and made Paine march down Main Street while reading aloud his letter of resignation several times. At no point did the crowd physically abuse Paine. They forcefully insisted he resign his position, but they never devolved into an unruly mob. Rev. Ebenezer Parkman noted in his diary, "P.M. am informed that a great multitude, above 1500, assembled at Worcester and oblige Honorable *Timothy Paine* to renounce his Commission as a Counselor etc. And this afternoon they go from Worcester to Rutland, to oblige Col. *Murray* to do the like: but he is gone to Boston." John Murray was the next target, but since he was holed up in Boston and the patriots could not locate him, they published a letter in the Boston newspapers demanding his resignation. Murray refused, but he was never able to return to his home in Rutland as a consequence. Timothy Ruggles, the third counselor, was also away from his house, and he also ended up hiding out in Boston.

Tensions were beginning to mount, so much so that false rumors began to circulate, which prompted swift action by the Massachusetts Militias. Rev. Parkman captures the highly charged atmosphere in his diary:

September 2, 1774

This morning was ushered in with *Alarms from every* Quarter, to get ready and run down to *Boston* or *Cambridge*. The Contents Magazine of Powder at *Winter Hill* had been carryed off -- namely [550?] Barrells; by Treachery; etc. This is told as the Chief Affair. 72 of our Neighbours marched from *Gales* (tis said) by break of Day; and others are continuely going. My young man goes armed, with them. About 5 p.m. *Grafton* Company, nigh 80, under Capt. *Golding*, march by us. N.B. Squire *Whipple* here. Says he is ready to *sign* etc. It is a Day of peculiar Anxiety and Distress! Such as we have not had -- Will the Lord graciously look upon us; and grant us Deliverance -- for we would hope and trust in His Name! We send for Mrs. *Spring* and her two Children to be here with us, while her husband is gone with the People. *Breck* returned from *Lancaster*. At Eve we have most sorrowful News that Hostilitys have commenced at *Cambridge*, and that Six of our people are killed; that probably Some at least may be of *Westborough*. *Joshua Chamberlin* stood next (as it is related) to one that was slain. We have many Vague accounts and indeed are left in uncertaintys about Every Thing that has occurred. *Sutton* soldiers -- about 250, pass along by us -- but after midnight are returning by reason of a Contrary Report. Mr. *Zech. Hicks* stops here. Breck is employed in the night to cast Bulletts. A Watch at the Meeting House to guard the Town stock etc. Some Towns, we hear, have lost much of theirs, as *Dedham*, *Wrentham* etc.

September 3

Capt. *Benjamin Fay* came here between 2 and 3 o'Clock in the morn in much Concern and knew not what to do. After Light and through most of the forenoon, vague uncertain Reports. *Sutton* men that had gone to Deacon Wood, came back to go down the Road again. My son *Breck* with provisions, Bread, Meat, etc., Coats, Blanket etc., for it was rainy, rides down towards Cambridge to relieve *Asa Ware*, Mr. *Spring*, and others who were unprovided. About noon the *Sutton* Companys come back again and go home, Rev. Chaplin among them. So do the *Grafton* men. Mr. *Abraham Temple* relates to me, that he, having been as far as to Cambridge and himself Seen many of the Transactions, that there were no Regulars there, no Artillery, no body Slain -- but that Lt. Gov. *Oliver*, Messrs. *Danforth*, *Joseph Lee*, Col. *Phips* (the high Sheriff) had resigned and promised that they would not act as Counsellors -- that Mr. Samuel *Winthrop* computed there were about 7000 of the Country people had gathered into *Cambridge* on this Occasion -- that it was probable, as he (Mr.

Temple) conceived, that the Troubles would subside. N.B. When the Sun run low, Our Company returned (consisting of Horse and Foot about 150). With them were my Son and my young man -- all without any Evil Occurrance. To God be Praise and Glory! I Suppose Capt. Maynard and those who were with him are returned also.

This event later became known as the "Powder Alarm," which started when a rumor circulated that the British had fired off a bombardment on Boston, had killed six men, and were now on the march. None of this information turned out to be true, but tens of thousands of men mobilized to protect Cambridge and Boston.

* * *

Everyone knew that there could be possible military confrontation in Worcester on September 6, so this time there was no need to call an alarm for militias to gather and head to the county seat. Rev. Parkman noted the day before,

> Another *Town Meeting*, upon our public Difficultys -- they agree to go to *Worcester tomorrow*, as it is expected that all other Towns of this County will, to prevent the session of the *Court* under the new unconstitutional Establishment -- and talk of Superseding the necessity of Courts by resolving upon having as few Cases as may be, and by Choosing men from among our Selves that may judge and determine Causes.

The men from Westborough most likely rose before dawn and then marched to Worcester that same morning. Parkman wrote in his diary on Sept. 6: "A great Company march with staves and Fife, under Capt. *Maynard*, to *Worcester*." The men of Westborough marched without guns, only "staves and Fife," because word that General Gage had changed his mind and had decided not to send troops into heavily armed Worcester

County, where they would have been vastly outnumbered, had reached the town before they left. Other companies hid their arms at the outskirts of town once they received the message that they would not be needed.

The gathered crowd forced the closure of the Inferior Court of Common Pleas and the Court of General Sessions, which effectively shut down British rule in Worcester County. Rev. Parkman noted, "I don't understand that there was any Disorder. Tis said the people behaved with Silence Decency & in good order." No one led the uprising. The group as a whole made all decisions in a reasoned, non-violent manner, which they were all used to doing in their town meetings. They simply insisted that the two dozen court officials resign their position, and with so many people standing outside of Daniel Heywood's tavern where the officials had convened and waited to hear their fate, they had little choice.

After the letters of resignation were signed, the militiamen from the various towns lined Main Street in Worcester in formation for a quarter mile, with Westborough grouped second in line from the front of the courthouse. The officials were then made to walk down the street and back with their hats in hand—reversing the traditional sign of deference—and to read aloud to each company the statement they had just signed that disavowed both their position and British authority over the courts. Tory Protesters who were not officials of the court were also rounded up and made to walk the gauntlet while reading their resignations from power. From here on out, the British never exercised control over Worcester County.

After shutting down the courts in Worcester, with the exception of Boston (where British soldiers were in a position to protect the judges) colonists proceeded to shut down the courts in every county seat in Massachusetts, including Salem, Concord, Barnstable, Taunton, and Plymouth counties. By the end of 1774, Massachusetts was, for the most part, no longer in the hands of the British.

Rev. Ebenezer Parkman

Rev. Ebenezer Parkman's son, Breck, was among the Westborough militiamen who attended the insurgence in Worcester. He cataloged the number of people who attended from each town and then passed this information on to his father. Rev. Parkman entered the numbers into his diary, which is why we have an exact accounting of how many people attended the mass uprising and from where: 4,622 from 37 towns. The numbers represented half the adult male population of the county, with Westborough's share of men totaling 200.

Even though Breck sided with the patriots by signing the covenant to boycott British goods and joined in the march to Worcester, Rev. Parkman himself was more cautious. He was not a Loyalist, but he tended to drag his feet when asked to take action in support of resistance to British rule. As we have already seen, Parkman was visited repeatedly by members of the Committee of Correspondence asking him to sign on to the boycott of British goods, or at least express his opinion on the matter. Over and over again, he delayed giving them a solid answer and was particularly worried about Governor Gage's proclamation that he would punish anyone who signed it. During a time when ministers tended to set the tone for their town's embrace or rejection of British authority, Westborough seems to be unusual in that the people pulled their minister along with them in their support of rebellion, rather than the other way around. Rev. Parkman was not uninterested in politics. He closely followed the events unfolding in Boston and expressed a desire for them to be resolved with the help of God. But he was much more concerned with following the rule of law than in subscribing to a higher principle of justice. Perhaps he thought that as minister of the town he had more to lose than anyone else, so he needed to be more careful.

September 1774.

5. Another Town meeting, upon o.r public difficultys — they agree to go to Worcester tomorrow as it is expected y.t all other Towns of this County will to prevent y.e Session of Court under y.e new unconstitutional Establishm.t — and talk of Superseding y.e Necessity of Courts by resolving upon having as few Cases as may be, & by choosing men from among o.r S. y.t may judge & determine Causes. Squire Whipple & several others sign the Agreem.t — Mr. Webb dines with us.

6. A g.t Company march.d w.th Staves & Fife und.r Capt. Maynard, to Worcester. Mr. Cornelius Waters from Dartmouth Col. dines with us. Read Considerations on y.e present measures with y.e Colonies.

7. Breck gives me acc.t y.t yesterday there assembled at Worcester 4722 Persons w.o were in arrangem.t und.r their particular Heads, leading each Town, but without Arms: Those Heads treated with y.e Judges & other Officers of y.e Court. The Court House was fill.d with Com.tees of Correspondence from each Town, & y.e Door fasten.d & guarded. The Court walk.d from Hayward's Tavern to y.e Court House [between the Ranks,] w.th their Hatts off; and then back; a Paper being Read, Signifying that y.y w.d Endeav.r & — but this not Satisfying, ano.r was drawn, & Read promiss.g y.t y.y would not Sit in that or any other Court und.r y.e new Regul.n by y.e late Acts of Parliam.t — I dont understand that there was any Disorder. The List stands thus,

[left margin note] ^ between the Ranks,

[left margin note] N.B. This, except Worcester & Spencer, is y.e order in w.ch y.e Company's Stood from y.e Court House & Southward. viz. Uxbridge first, Westboro second &c. a few Company's had Arms

Worcester	260	Princetown	60	Palmer	38
Uxbridge	156	Harvard	103	Sutton	500
Westborough	200	Hubbardston	55	Westminster	120
Rutland	130	Lunenbourg	40	Oxford Troop	40
Athol	51	Western	100	N. Shrewbury	100
Royalston	39	Winchenden	45	S. Shrewbury	135
New Braintry	140	Southboro	35	Northboro	85
Brookfield	216	Chauxitt	200	Oxford	80
Duglass	130	Leicester	180	Oakham	50
Grafton	210	Spencer	164	Petersham	70
Holden	100	Sturbridge	150	Paxton	80
Hardwick	220	Bolton	100	Upton	100
				Templeton	120
					4722

Ebenezer Parkman, *Diary*, September 5-7, 1774
(America Antiquarian Society)

The year of 1774 was full of events and change for both Westborough and Massachusetts. On December 31, Rev. Parkman laments during his reflections on the year:

> Through the Long-suffering of God I am brought to the Close of another Year. The Occurrences of it have been very remarkable: Especially by the Changes in the Civil Government -- Governor *Hutchinson* gone to *England*, Governor *Gage* in his Room. The General Court is moved to *Salem*, which is made the chief Seat of Government. The Counsellors made by *Mandamus*. General Court soon dissolved. The Company of Cadets resign and are disbanded: Boston port blocked up by men of War: the Common, the Neck, and Fort-Hill have 5 Regiments. The *Continental Congress*, and the *Provincial* meet, one at *Philadelphia* Sept. 5, the other *Concord* and *Cambridge*. The Towns in Confusion by Reason that the Superior and Inferior Courts cease. Mobs and Riots; *Whigs* and *Torys* -- as if our Happiness *were nigh to an End*! O God save us!

The British Point of View

England saw how local government in Massachusetts was insufficient in both preventing the Boston Tea Party and in pursuing the prosecution of the perpetrators. From their point of view, the passage of the Intolerable Acts of 1774 was merely an attempt to restore a balance between the government and the people that was put into place by the Glorious Revolution back in 1688. British troops were unavailable to put down the Tea Party insurrection, so Parliament passed a quartering act. The Council of Massachusetts refused to call on troops to protect the ships and their cargo, so now it was to be replaced by a body appointed by the King. Insurrection was planned during town meetings, so now those meetings would have to be sanctioned by the British government. All of these changes were aimed at thwarting the revolutionary movement, not at subverting democracy, but that is exactly what the laws did and how the people perceived them.

From the British perspective, the rebels who closed down the Worcester courts broke the law; but from the rebels' perspective, they were defending a higher law of self-determination. Despite General Gage's threats to close down town meetings, these meetings continued to take place across Massachusetts, and every time Gage tried to use force to institute order, thousands of farmers appeared and forced Gage's troops to withdraw. Gage would have liked to have deployed troops throughout the colony to put down the rebellion, but with each town heavily armed and prepared for battle, he did not dare to do so. He knew that he had a revolution on his hands, and so did King George. In November of 1774, George III acknowledged, "The New England Governments are in a State of Rebellion, and blows must decide whether they are to be subject to this Country or Independent."

King George III, by Johann Zoffany, 1771
(Royal Collection Trust)

After the overthrow of the courts in Worcester and other counties, a Provincial Congress was established. It advised towns to stop submitting tax payments to the British and instead redirect them to the new legislative body in order to procure arms and establish military structures. By the spring of 1775, the people of Massachusetts had put in place a shadow government that acted in the absence of British authority. There was no going back to British rule now.

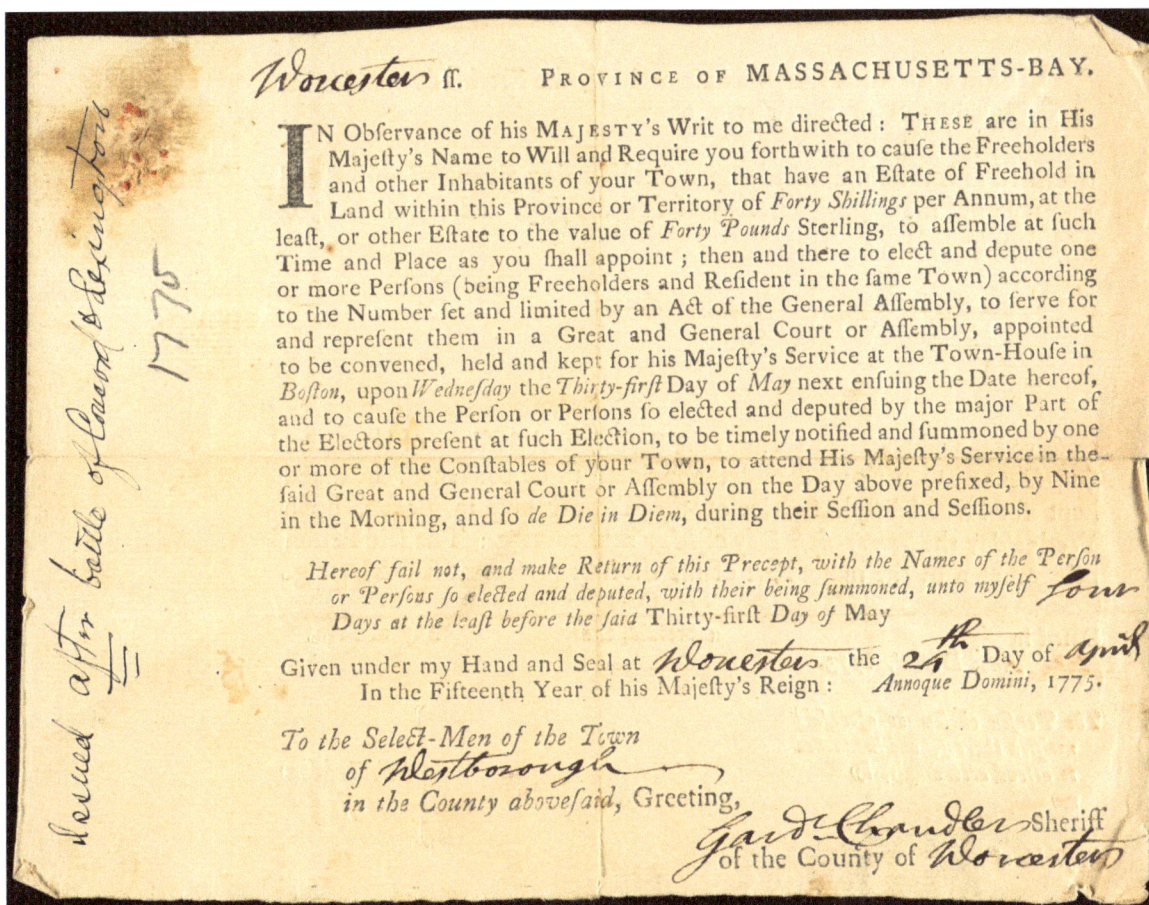

Call for Representation on the General Court from the British Government, April 24, 1775, after the alternative Provincial Congress had already been established (front)
(Digital Commonwealth/Westborough Public Library)

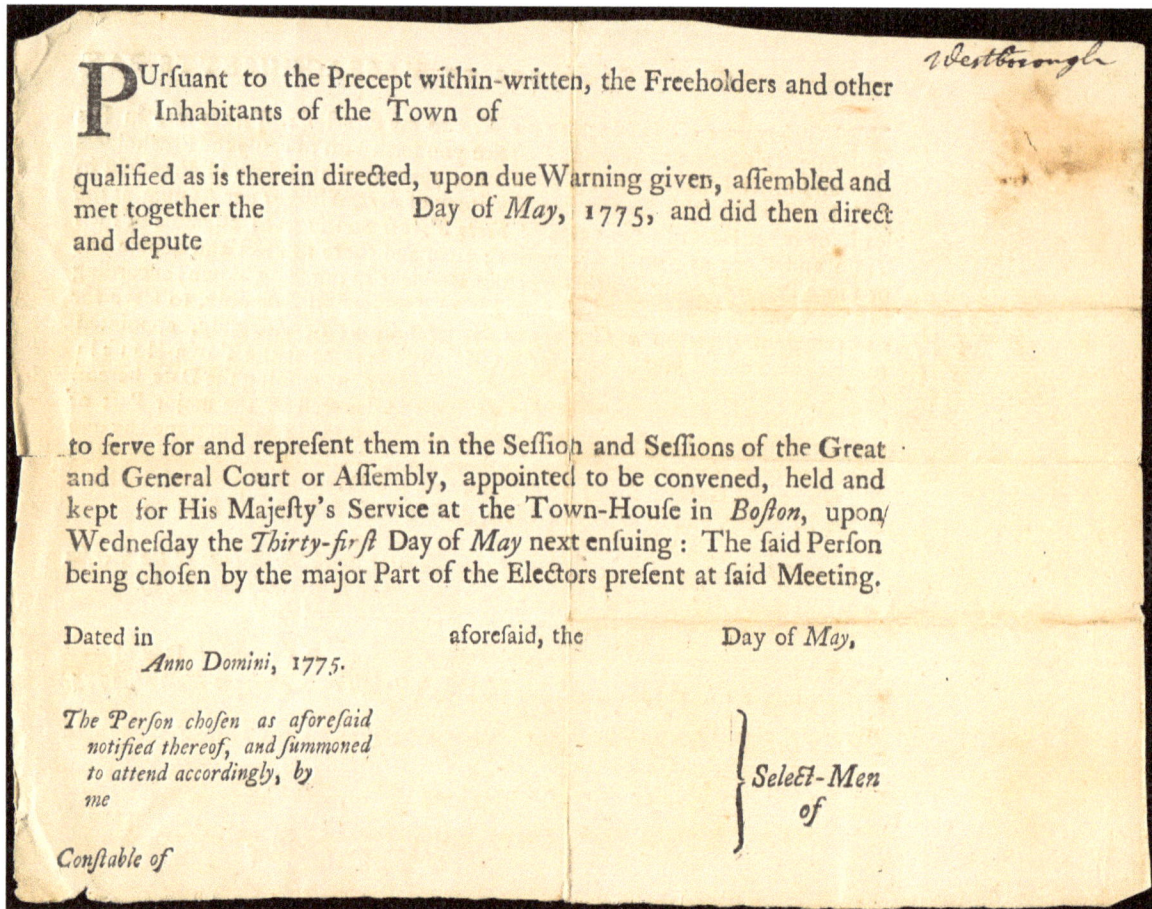

PUrsuant to the Precept within-written, the Freeholders and other Inhabitants of the Town of

qualified as is therein directed, upon due Warning given, assembled and met together the   Day of *May*, 1775, and did then direct and depute

to serve for and represent them in the Session and Sessions of the Great and General Court or Assembly, appointed to be convened, held and kept for His Majesty's Service at the Town-House in *Boston*, upon Wednesday the *Thirty-first* Day of *May* next ensuing : The said Person being chosen by the major Part of the Electors present at said Meeting.

Dated in   aforesaid, the   Day of *May*,
     Anno Domini, 1775.

The *Person chosen as aforesaid notified thereof, and summoned to attend accordingly, by me*

                               Select-Men of

Constable of

Call for Representation on the General Court from the British Government, April 24, 1775 (back) – note that Westborough ignored the call and never filled in the blanks on the form (Digital Commonwealth/Westborough Public Library)

Westborough's Move Towards Independence

From this point forward, the story of the American Revolution is more familiar. On April 19, 1775, the British marched to Lexington and Concord to capture colonial military supplies. Westborough's minutemen received the call and gathered at the Gale Tavern before marching to Concord (although they never saw action because they were too late). In many people's eyes, these events signify the start of the Revolution, mostly because they were battles. We do not normally think that revolution can happen through a peaceful (yet forceful) overthrow of a government, but that is precisely what happened in Worcester, with Westborough helping to lead the charge.

While the rest of the American colonies moved towards independence, the new Massachusetts House of Representatives passed a resolve on May 10, 1776 asking that

> the inhabitants of each Town in this Colony ought, in full meeting warned for that purpose, to advise the person or persons who shall be chosen to represent them in the next General Court whether that, if the honourable Congress should, for the safety of the said Colonies, declare them independent of the Kingdom of Great Britain, they, the said inhabitants, will solemnly engage, with their lives and fortunes, to support them in the measure.

Would the towns, in other words, support a declaration of independence from Great Britain?

At a town meeting on May 24 "to Consider of a Resolve of the House of Representatives on May ye 10, 1776 concerning Indepentcy," Westborough "Voted to advise Capt Stephen Maynard our Representative to Conform to Said Resolve in Case that the Honourable Congress Shall Judge it most

Expedient for the Safety and wellfair of the Colony." This vote served as Westborough's ratification of independence from Great Britain.

Detail from *Town Meeting Records*, May 24, 1776 – Westborough's response to the question of independence posited by the Massachusetts House of Representatives on May 10, 1776 (Westborough Town Clerk's Office)

The Declaration of Independence

By the time the Continental Congress met in Philadelphia to declare freedom from Great Britain in 1776, Westborough and other Massachusetts towns had been operating under their own system of government separate from the British for almost two years. After the copy of the Declaration of Independence arrived in Westborough from Salem, MA (where it was printed for distribution to Massachusetts towns), Westborough followed the orders printed at the bottom:

> ORDERED, That the Declaration of Independence be printed ; and a Copy sent to the Ministers of each Parish, of every Denomination, within this State. ; and that they severally be *required* to read the same to their respective Congregations, as soon as divine Service is ended, in the Afternoon, on the first Lord's-Day after they have received it :--And after such Publication thereof, to deliver the said Declaration to the Clerks of their several Towns, or Districts ; who are hereby required to record the same in their respective Town, or District Books, there to remain as a *perpetual* MEMORIAL thereof.

Rev. Ebenezer Parkman dutifully read the Declaration aloud to the congregation on August 25, 1776. Characteristically, when Northborough's minister read the Declaration, preached a lecture, and planned other "Great Doings . . . on that Occasion," Parkman, though invited, decided not to attend the celebrations. After Parkman read the founding document to the people of Westborough, it was then copied into the town records.

The closing of the courts in Worcester in 1774 reverberated not only throughout the thirteen colonies and across the ocean to Great Britain but throughout the world and up until today, with the form of democracy that resulted continuing to serve as a standard bearer. The American Revolution was not an uprising of peasants against their oppressors. It was the product of free, middle-class farmers who were scared of losing their land and their way of life, of people acting to preempt possible exploitation against their will. The Revolution did not start as an effort to create something new. Rather, the people were forced to create a new system of government in order to protect what they had. In this respect, it was a conservative revolution aimed at preservation rather than radical alteration.

But in many ways, revolution is embedded within the system of government that resulted: we get to vote our leaders in and out of office; the people of Westborough still get to go to town meeting and have their say about what happens in the town; and we get to run for office and thereby directly shape the society in which we live.

With the closing of the courts in Worcester, people who once thought of themselves as British-Americans now had to forge a new identity. Through the collective act of holding militia days—both before marching into Worcester and afterward—the people were participating in the creation of that identity and a new set of loyalties that no longer included Great Britain.

The Declaration of Independence as copied into the
***Town Meeting Records*, 1776**
(Westborough Town Clerk's Office)

Epilogue: How is Today Different?

Even though the expression "history repeats itself" is a cliché, that does not mean it is true. The following images depict themes that appear in *The Rebellion Begins*, but as you think about how they relate to what you have just read, do not settle for the similarities. Those are too easy to spot. Instead, try to tease out the differences between the then and now, and then think about *why* they are different and *how* we got here.

Town Meetings

Westborough continues to function under a town meeting form of government. Since the town was founded in 1717, Selectmen have been ordering warrants for town meetings to be drawn up by the Town Clerk and then posted, so that people can anticipate the issues that will both be discussed and put up for a direct vote by members of the town.

The two town meeting warrants that appear on the following pages involve the election of officers. The 1775 special town meeting warrant calls for the town to gather at the Meeting House to select a representative to the Provincial Court, and the 2017 warrant calls for people first to vote for town officers on March 7, 2017, and then to meet on March 18, 2017, at the Westborough High School to conduct town business. The 1775 warrant also calls for a vote on whether to allow people who cannot work off their highway taxes to do so the following year, whereas the 2017 warrant contains 42 articles and goes on for 35 pages.

Note that even though the position of constable no longer formally exists in Westborough, the town meeting warrant for 2017 still calls on constables to spread the word that a meeting is taking place, much like the 1775 warrant does. Nowadays, the town website mostly serves this function. The antiquated language that continues to appear in town meeting warrants is a sign of how deep the tradition of holding town-wide meetings runs. But Westborough is now debating whether or not to continue its town meeting form of government, since attendance at town meetings lately makes up only a tiny subset of the 18,000 who live in town and since the issues that the town faces are often complex. How long will Westborough be able to carry on the tradition of town meeting with its growing population, and at what point does the tradition no longer serve the needs of the town?

Special Westborough Town Meeting Warrant, June 26, 1775
(Digital Commonwealth/Westborough Public Library)

COMMONWEALTH OF MASSACHUSETTS
WORCESTER, SS

TO ANY CONSTABLE IN THE TOWN OF WESTBOROUGH, IN THE COUNTY OF WORCESTER, GREETINGS:

In the name of the Commonwealth of Massachusetts, you are directed to notify and warn the inhabitants of the Town of Westborough, qualified to vote in elections and town affairs, to meet in various precincts in Westborough on Tuesday, the 7th day of March, 2017 at 7:00 A.M. for the following purposes:

ARTICLE 1: Annual Town Election (Board of Selectmen)
To bring in their votes for:

One	(1)	Selectman (3 years)
One	(1)	Town Moderator (3 years)
One	(1)	Town Clerk (3 years)
One	(1)	Planning Board member (5 years)
One	(1)	Planning Board member (1 year)
Two	(2)	School Committee members (3 years)
Three	(3)	Trustees of Public Library (3 years)

Polls will be open from 7 A.M. to 8 P.M. in the following places:

Precincts 1 – 5 Westborough High School, 90 West Main Street

And to act on the following articles at the adjourned session of said meeting on March 18, 2017, at 1:00 P.M. in the Westborough High School Auditorium and Gymnasium on West Main Street.

The Town Manager's Statements printed in italics are not part of the formal articles of the warrant. They constitute additional information offered for the benefit of the voters, true and correct as of the time of posting of the warrant, but subject to change as called for. They are not to be construed so as to broaden or limit the scope of the formal articles.

ARTICLE 2: Town Reports (Advisory Finance Committee)
To see if the Town will vote to hear the reports of the several town officers and committees, and to dissolve any committees established by Town Meeting that have fulfilled their mission, or take any other action thereon.

ARTICLE 3: Prior Years Bills (Country Club Operating Committee)
To see if the Town will vote to transfer from the Country Club Reserve Account the sum of Five Hundred Ninety Three and 90/100 Dollars ($593.90) for the purpose of paying outstanding balances in the Superintendent's contracts in FY14; FY15; and FY16, or take any other action thereon.

1

First page (out of 35) of the Westborough Town Meeting Warrant posted on February 28, 2017.
(Town of Westborough)

Farms

Only a few farms are active in Westborough today, but they have a long history and are a constant reminder of the town's agricultural roots. Even so, the farms of today function much differently than they did in the past, and innovation is key to their future. Today, sales outlets are much more diverse. The farms in Westborough not only sell directly to consumers with farm stands, pick-your-own fields, participation in local farmer's markets, and Community Supported Agriculture (CSA) programs, but they also sell to local restaurants and other wholesale outlets.

Advertisement for the Nourse Farm Heritage Day, June 17, 2017.
(Nourse Farm, Westborough)

Innovation does not stop with the sale of produce. Many Westborough farms advertise with websites, e-mail newsletters, and social media. Some farms have expanded to include gift barns, plant sales, and resources for home gardeners. At least one farm even harvests energy from the sun with blocks of solar panels. Innovation is crucial to the success of local farming, and if farming continued as it did in the colonial period, a "Farm Heritage Day" would make little sense. Why is innovation such a necessity for these farms?

Westborough farms are local, not international like the farms were in colonial America or big industrial farms in the Midwest are today. Westborough recognizes the importance of its farms and has measures in place to encourage buyers of farm property to continue using the land for such a purpose. Why does the town need to take action to make sure that local farms continue into the future? How do local farms contribute to the overall quality of life of a community today?

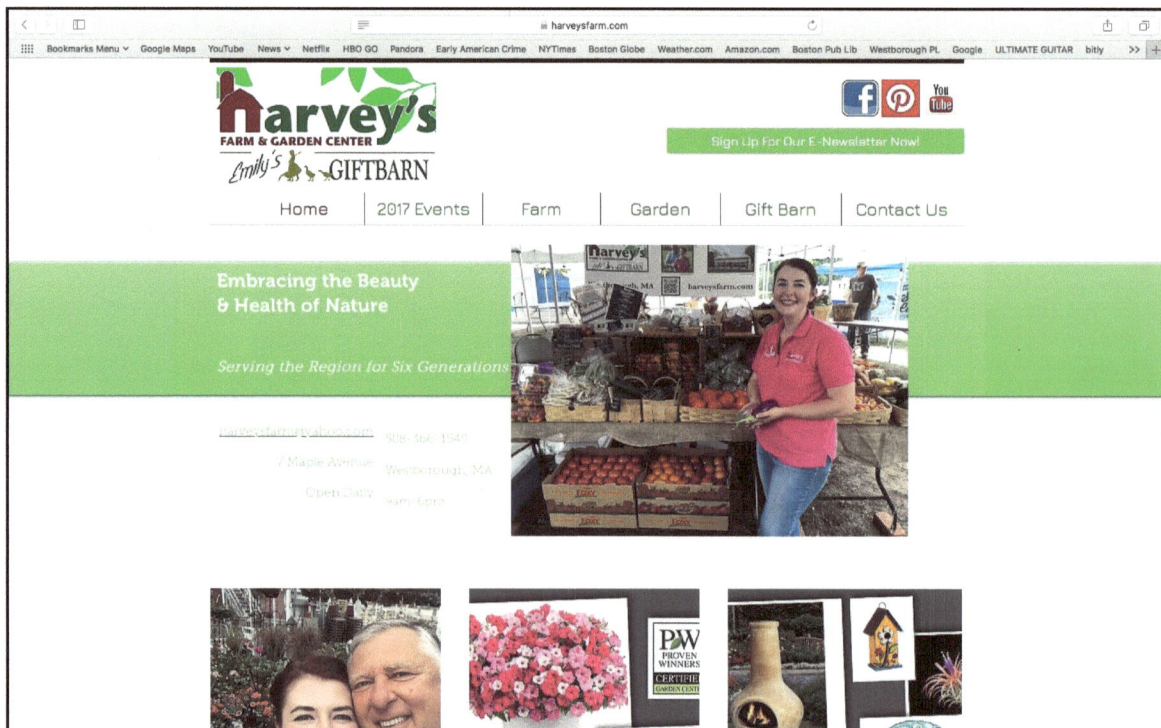

Website screen shot from harveysfarm.com, August 31, 2017
(Harvey's Farm, Westborough)

Boycotts

Just like in 1774, consumers today use the power of the purse to protest actions that they perceive to be unjust, with the theory being that if they stop buying certain products, they can pressure a company to change course. The first image below comes from Boycott Black Thursday, a movement that protests stores opening on Thanksgiving Day to get a jump-start on "Black Friday" sales. The movement argues that opening stores on this national holiday not only forces employees to have to work on a day they traditionally have off, but also violates the spirit of a day meant to give thanks for what we already have. The protest seems to have been effective, because many "big box" stores gave in to the pressure and decided to close their stores on Thanksgiving Day in 2016.

Facebook image from BoycottBlackThursday, October 27, 2017
(Facebook)

Withholding business to elicit change is not limited to consumers. On June 11, 2017, Bank of America announced that it was withdrawing its support of a Shakespeare in the Park production of Shakespeare's *Julius Caesar* by the Public Theater in New York City. The production cast an actor who resembled President Donald Trump in the lead role. Naturally, the character is stabbed to death on stage, as is called for both by history and by Shakespeare. The withdrawal of funding by Bank of America shows that just as consumers can protest company decisions through boycotts, companies can protest actions that they deem inappropriate by pulling back their money as well.

Boycotting the drinking of tea not only cut into British company profits, but it galvanized the colonies against British authority. Do boycotts today produce similar ends?

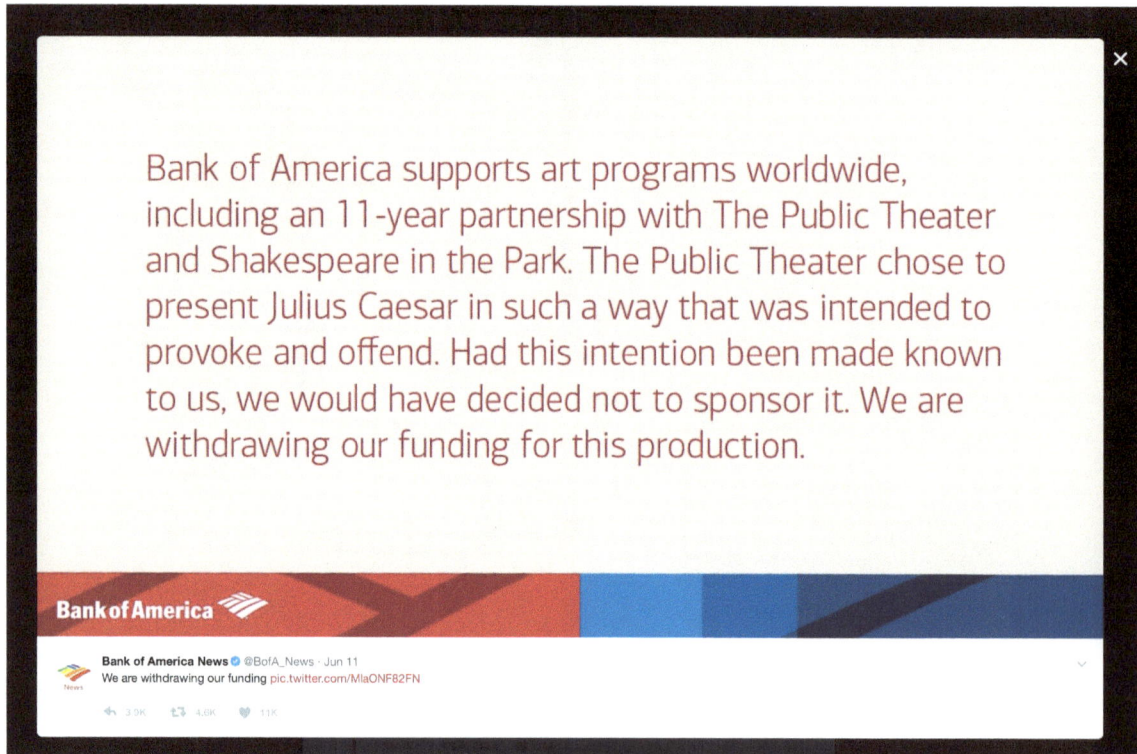

Bank of America supports art programs worldwide, including an 11-year partnership with The Public Theater and Shakespeare in the Park. The Public Theater chose to present Julius Caesar in such a way that was intended to provoke and offend. Had this intention been made known to us, we would have decided not to sponsor it. We are withdrawing our funding for this production.

Bank of America Tweet announcing its withdrawal of funding for a production of *Julius Caesar*, June 11, 2017
(Twitter)

Taverns

You no longer declare your political allegiance by walking into a tavern in Westborough, as was the case in 1774 when the owner usually set the establishment's royalist or rebel leanings. While political discussions surely take place in the taverns and bars of Westborough today, conversation is more likely to turn to the safer topic of sports, where disagreements are less likely to elicit hard feelings (unless, of course, you loudly declare loyalty to the New York Yankees). Even so, Westborough currently does not support a self-defined sports bar, which has become a highly popular bar theme in other towns and parts of the country. If we turned off the games on our televisions to have spirited political discussion over a beer every now and then, would our nation's politics be less divisive, or would bars inevitably end up polarized like they were in 1774?

Interior view of the Westborough House of Pizza bar, 2017
(Yelp)

Sign for the Central House Tavern and Restaurant in Westborough, 2017
(Author photo)

Revolution

The power of the people to effect change was the driving force behind the American Revolution, and the system of government that was subsequently put into place was meant to ensure that the people continue to maintain this power. But with such power comes great responsibility. The foundation of our political system is the understanding that everyone living in the United States has an obligation to educate himself or herself and to participate in the functioning of our civil society. When we believe that government is not serving our interests and is controlled by other entities, is it the system that is lacking or the fact that we have allowed others to make decisions for us due to our own passivity? When politicians offer up "revolution," what kind of revolution are they truly offering? And when we vote, are we seeking to upend the system, make improvements to our lives through progressive political change, or simply preserve our current way of life?

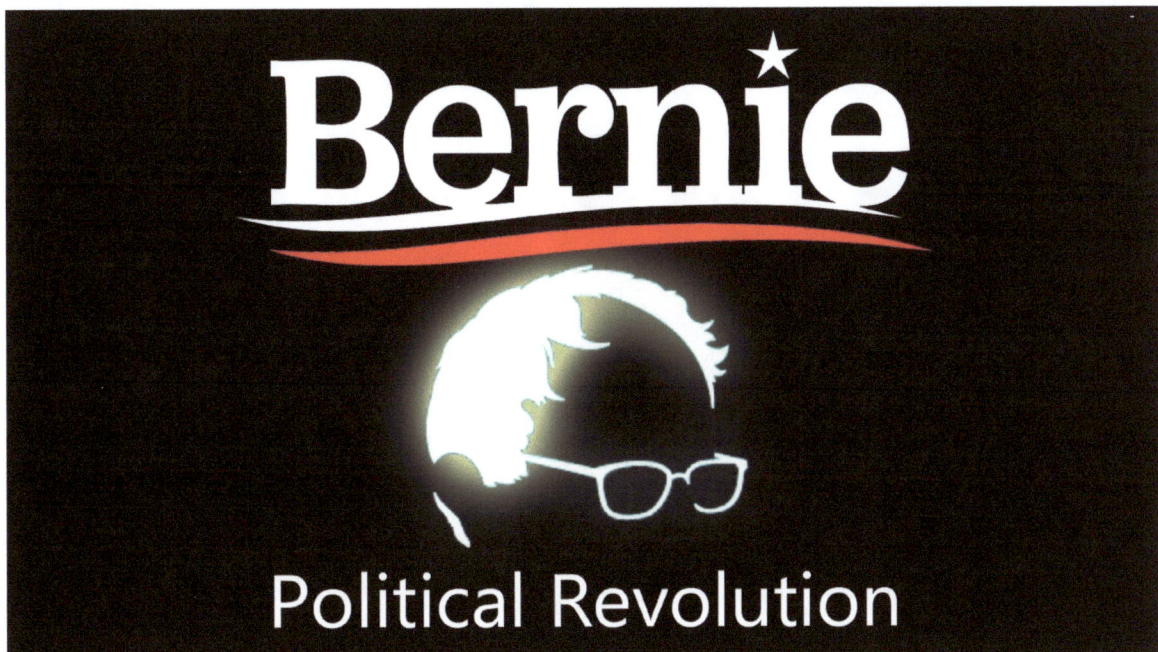

Donald Trump and Bernie Sanders campaign graphics, 2016

Community Celebrations

Militia training days had a serious purpose but were also gatherings that celebrated the cohesion of communities. Today, some of us honor the men and women who took the first steps toward founding our country by dressing in colonial period clothing and recreating the times in which they lived in an attempt to better understand the decisions that they made. At the time of the writing of this book, Westborough is celebrating its 300th anniversary as a town. The many programs and events scheduled to celebrate the town's history throughout the year is evidence that the spirit that brought the people of Westborough together back then is just as strong today.

Militia Unit
(Col. Bailey's 2nd Massachusetts Unit)

Westborough is a different place now than it was back in 1774. While we honor all that unites us with the people back then, we also celebrate the differences that define the town as it exists today.

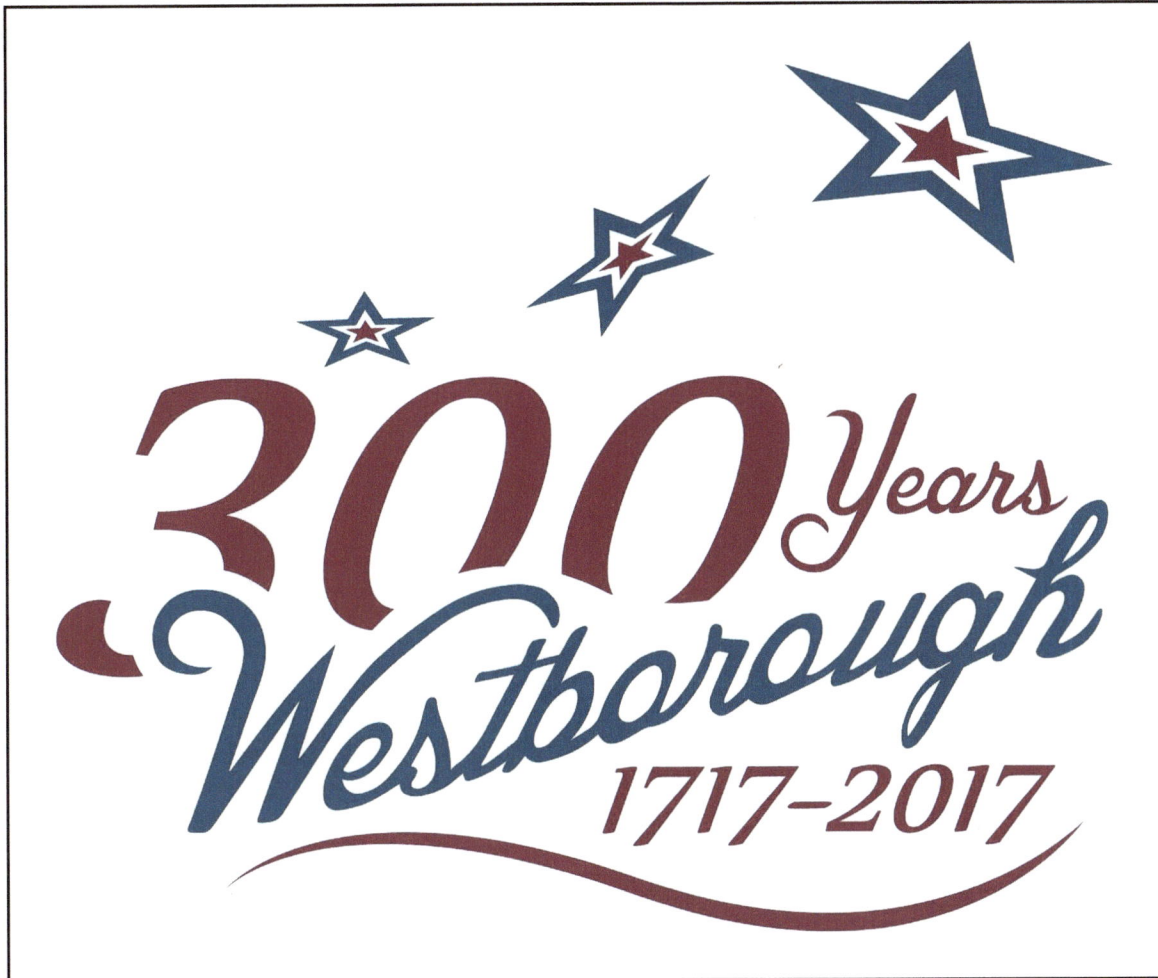

Logo for the Westborough 300th Anniversary Celebration

Sources

Adams, John. Letter to Thomas Jefferson, 24 August 1815. *Founders Archive*. National Archives. https://founders.archives.gov/documents/Jefferson/03-08-02-0560.

Allen, Kristina Nilson. *On the Beaten Path: Westborough, Massachusetts*. Westborough: Westborough Civic Club and Westborough Historical Society, 1984.

American Archives: Consisting of a Collection of Authentick Records, State Papers, Debates, and Letters and Other Notices of Publick Affairs. Peter Force, comp. Vol. 6. Washington: M. St. Clair Clarke and Peter Force, 1846. Internet Archive: https://archive.org/details/americanarchives06forcuoft.

Beales, Jr., Ross W. "'The present Torrent of Liberty is irresitable': From Revival to Revolution in Westborough, Massachusetts." Paper Presented at the Conference on Awakenings and Revivals in American History, Liberty University, April 16-18, 2009.

Blackburn, Marc K. *Interpreting American Military History at Museums and Historic Sites*. Interpreting History Series. New York: Rowman & Littlefield, 2016.

Brown, Richard D. "Massachusetts Towns Respond to the Boston Committee of Correspondence, 1773." *William and Mary Quarterly*, Vol. 25, No. 1 (Jan. 1968), pp. 22-39.

DeForest, Heman Packard. *The History of Westborough, Massachusetts*. Part I. The Early History. Westborough, 1891.

Sources

Forbes, Harriette Merrifield. *The Hundredth Town: Glimpses of Life in Westborough, 1717-1817*. Boston: Press of Rockwell and Churchill, 1889.

Gildrie, Richard P. "Defiance, Diversion, and the Exercise of Arms: The Several Meanings of Colonial Training Days in Colonial Massachusetts." *Military Affairs*, Vol. 52, No. 2 (Apr., 1988), pp. 53-55.

Howell, William Huntting. "Entering the Lists: The Politics of Ephemera in Eastern Massachusetts, 1774." *Early American Studies*, Vol. 9, No. 1 (Winter 2011), pp. 187-217.

Mook, H. Telfer. "Training Day in New England." *The New England Quarterly*, Vol. 11, No. 4 (Dec., 1938), pp. 675-697.

More Old Houses in Westborough, Mass. and Vicinity with Their Occupants. Westborough: The Westborough Historical Society, 1908.

Newcomer, Lee Nathaniel. "Yankee Rebels of Inland Massachusetts." *The William and Mary Quarterly*, Vol. 9, No. 2 (Apr., 1952), pp. 156-165.

Nelson, William E. "The Legal Restraint of Power in Pre-Revolutionary America: Massachusetts as a Case Study, 1760-1775." *The American Journal of Legal History*, Vol. 18, No. 1 (Jan., 1974), pp. 1-32.

Parkman, Ebenezer. Diary, 1774. Transcribed by Ross W. Beales, Jr.

---. *The Diary of Ebenezer Parkman, 1703-1782*. First Part of Three Volumes in One, 1719-1755. Ed. Francis G. Walett. Worcester: American Antiquarian Society, 1974.

Radabaugh, Jack S. "The Militia of Colonial Massachusetts." *Military Affairs*, Vol. 18, No. 1 (Spring, 1954), pp. 1-18.

Raphael, Ray. *The First American Revolution: Before Lexington and Concord*. New York: The New Press, 2002.

---. *A People's History of the American Revolution: How Common People Shaped the Fight for Independence*. New York: The New Press, 2016.

---. "Worcester, Lexington, and the American Revolution: Debunking the Myth of the 'Shot Heard 'Round the World.'" *Historical Journal of Massachusetts*, Vol. 45, No. 2 (Summer, 2017), pp. 2-33.

Raphael, Ray and Marie Raphael. *The Spirit of '74: How the American Revolution Began*. New York: The New Press, 2015.

Sismondo, Christine. *America Walks into a Bar: A Spirited History of Taverns and Saloons, Speakeasies and Grog Shops*. New York: Oxford UP, 2011.

Some Old Houses in Westborough, Mass. and Their Occupants. Westborough: The Westborough Historical Society, 1906.

Sosin, Jack M. "The Massachusetts Acts of 1774: Coercive or Preventive?" *Huntington Library Quarterly*, Vol. 26, No. 3 (May, 1963), pp. 235-252.

York, Neil L. "Imperial Impotence: Treason in 1774 Massachusetts." *Law and History Review*, Vol. 29, No. 3 (August 2011), pp. 657-701.